KEYS *for* LEADERSHIP

DR. MYLES MUNROE

KEYS for LEADERSHIP

WHITAKER
HOUSE

KEYS FOR LEADERSHIP

ISBN-13: 978-1-60374-029-6
ISBN-10: 1-60374-029-5
Printed in the United States of America
© 2008 by Dr. Myles Munroe

Whitaker House
1030 Hunt Valley Circle
New Kensington, PA 15068
www.whitakerhouse.com

Library of Congress Cataloging-in-Publication Data

Munroe, Myles.
Keys for leadership / Myles Munroe.
p.   cm.
ISBN 978-1-60374-029-6 (pbk. : alk. paper) 1. Leadership—Religious aspects—Christianity—
Miscellanea. I. Title.
BV4597.53.L43M85 2008
158'.4—dc22   2007046551

1 2 3 4 5 6 7 8 9 10 11 12 ᴜᴊ 16 15 14 13 12 11 10 09 08

INTRODUCTION

*E*very human being was created to lead in an area of gifting. This means the Creator designed you to fulfill a specific purpose and assignment in life, and your assignment determines your area of leadership.

The ability to fulfill this assignment, however, begins with developing a leadership mind-set. When you think according to the spirit of leadership, you begin the process of becoming a leader. Some of the unique attitudes or qualities of leaders include passion, initiative, teamwork, innovation, persistence, discipline, time management, confidence, positive disposition, patience, peace, and compassion.

When the spirit of leadership comes alive within someone, it produces an attitude that transforms that person from a follower into a leader. It also takes those who are in leadership positions into a realm of leadership they never before have experienced.

Meditate on the following *Keys for Leadership* and develop a spirit of leadership as you move forward in fulfilling your special, God-given assignment on earth.

—*Dr. Myles Munroe*

Introduction to Keys *for* Leadership

$\mathscr{T}$rapped within every follower is
a hidden leader.

The most important quality of true leadership is the spirit of leadership. All humans inherently possess the leadership spirit, but only those who capture the *spirit* of leadership ever become truly effective leaders.

True leaders are distinguished by a unique mental attitude that emanates from an internalized discovery of self. This creates self-worth and a strong, positive, confident self-concept.

$\mathscr{E}$very human has the instinct and capacity for leadership, but most do not have the courage or will to cultivate it.

$\mathcal{T}$rue leadership is a product of inspiration, not manipulation.

True leaders do not seek power, but are driven by a passion to achieve a noble cause.

*Y*our assignment determines your area of leadership. Deep inside each of us is a big dream struggling to free itself from the limitations of our past experiences, present circumstances, and self-imposed doubts.

Man's greatest ignorance is of himself. What you believe about yourself creates your world. No human can live beyond the limits of his or her beliefs.

*Y*our thoughts create your beliefs, your beliefs create your convictions, your convictions create your attitude, your attitude controls your perception, and your perception dictates your behavior.

$\mathcal{L}$eadership is a trusted privilege
given by followers.

*A*ll the money in the world can make you rich, and all the power in the world can make you strong, but these things can never make you a leader.

There is nothing as powerful as attitude. Attitude dictates your response to the present and determines the quality of your future. You are your attitude, and your attitude is you. If you do not control your attitude, it will control you.

Keys for Leadership

$\mathscr{T}$he distinguishing factor between a winner and a loser is attitude. More opportunities have been lost, withheld, and forfeited due to attitude than from any other cause. Attitude is a more powerful distinction in life than beauty, power, wealth, title, or social status.

*A*ttitude is a natural product of
the integration of self-worth, self-concept,
self-esteem, and sense of value or significance.
In essence, your attitude is the manifestation
of who you think you are.

No amount of training in leadership skills, courses in management methods, power titles, promotions, or associations can substitute for the right attitude.

*E*ach of us was created to rule, govern,
control, master, manage, and lead
our environments.

*Y*ou are in essence a leader, whether
you manifest it or not. Whether you are
rich, poor, young, old, male, female, black,
white, a citizen of an industrialized nation, a
citizen of a Third-World nation, educated, or
uneducated—you possess the nature
and capacity for leadership.

$\mathcal{B}$eing in the position of
a follower doesn't negate your inherent
leadership potential.

$\mathcal{L}$eadership is not an elite club for a certain few. It is the true essence of all human beings. Leadership is inherent in our nature and is fundamental to our origins, our human makeup, and our destiny.

$\mathcal{T}$rue leadership is an attitude that naturally inspires and motivates others, and it comes from an internalized discovery about yourself. You cannot "learn" an attitude. If someone learns an attitude, it's called conditioning or mere mental assent. That's not leadership.

KEYS for LEADERSHIP

*A*n attitude is a perspective, a motivation, or a desire that comes from within and is not based on a temporary external consequence. It is something deeply personal and internal that influences and transforms your thinking.

The key to the spirit of leadership is attitude rather than aptitude.

$\mathcal{M}$ost of us are not leaders today because, in our hearts, we don't believe that is who we are.

*B*ecause true leaders discover and understand who they are and what their purpose is, they influence their environments more than their environments influence them.

$\mathscr{T}$rue leaders strive to overcome crises and become creative in difficulty.

All of us must discover and cultivate the spirit of leadership—the attitude of shaping and forming our lives according to our purposes. We've been so conditioned by discouragement, failure, or the oppression of others that we are afraid to follow our natural leadership instincts.

$\mathcal{L}$eadership potential within you is waiting to be discovered. You were *born* to lead, but you must *become* a leader.

*T*rue leadership fundamentally requires
the responsibility of taking followers into
the exciting unknown and creating
a new reality for them.

$\mathcal{L}$eadership is the capacity to influence others through inspiration motivated by a passion, generated by a vision, produced by a conviction, ignited by a purpose.

People whom you inspire call you "leader" when they are stirred to participate in the positive vision that you are presenting them—whether it is the vision for a country, a company, or a cause.

*I*f inspiration is the key to legitimate influence and thus the source of true leadership, then inspiration should be the pursuit of all true leaders.

*T*rue leadership passion is the discovery of a belief, a reason, an idea, a conviction, or a cause—not just to live for, but also to die for—that focuses on benefiting mankind as a whole.

$\mathscr{T}$rue leaders are those who effectively express their inner passion, which finds a common response in the hearts of others. It is passion that attracts people to the leader who, in turn, motivates them to take action.

*T*he greatest leadership seems to surface during times of personal, social, economic, political, and spiritual conflict.

While leaders have followers, having followers is not a prerequisite for being a leader. The demands of leadership may require that you stand alone in the face of conflict, public opinion, or crisis.

When you have a purpose and a passion, you must act on it, even if you're the only one who believes in it at the time.

KEYS for LEADERSHIP

*I*nspiration is the divine deposit of destiny in the heart of a person.

True leaders discover keys to the nature of leadership from the examples of others, but they never try to become those other leaders. They must use their own gifts and abilities to do what they are individually called to do.

True leadership is first concerned with who you are, as opposed to what you do. Leadership action flows naturally from a personal leadership revelation.

The *leadership spirit* is the inherent leadership capacity and potential that is the essential nature of human beings. The *spirit of leadership* is the mind-set or attitudes that accompany a leadership spirit and allow dormant leadership potential to be fully manifested and maximized.

The inherent capacity of the human spirit to lead, manage, and dominate was placed there at the point of creation and made necessary by the purpose and assignment for which mankind was created.

The leadership spirit is the essence of the human spirit. Man doesn't *have* a spirit; man *is* a spirit, and that spirit is an expression of God's Spirit.

When we become our true selves, we will naturally be leaders.

*I*f we were created to be leaders, then
we must all possess the capacity, inherent
desire, natural talents, potential, and abilities
that correspond to being a leader. You
cannot demand from a product
what it does not possess.

KEYS for LEADERSHIP

The Creator is a leader-maker. Being designed in the image and likeness of God means that we were ordained by Him to be leaders. God's requirement that we have dominion is evidence that the ability to lead is inherent in every human spirit.

To exercise leadership, you must believe that you are inherently a leader.

$\mathcal{D}$o not seek greatness, but seek to serve others with your gift to the maximum extent that you can, and you will become a sought-after person. In essence, Jesus defined true leadership as becoming a person who is valuable to others rather than a person of just position or fame.

53

The shortest distance to leadership is service. Genuine leadership is not measured by how many people serve you, but by how many people you serve. The greater your service, the greater your value to others, and the greater your leadership.

$\mathcal{L}$oving money at the expense of the dignity, value, and welfare of others is an abuse of our *"power to get wealth"* (Deuteronomy 8:18).

$\mathcal{T}$rue leaders are honest. There is no manipulation or deception in their dealings with others or their pursuit of their visions. True leaders possess candor and a sense of self. They are true to themselves first and then to others.

The most important pursuit in life is the pursuit of truth.

*T*rue leaders are born in the presence of their Creator because that is where they discover the truth about themselves. To discover the truth about your ability and destiny, you must rediscover the value of a relationship with your Source.

$\mathcal{R}$ediscovering God as your Source
will naturally lead you to the revelation
that all humans are created in His image
and likeness, and therefore possess
the same value, worth, and
esteem that you do.

True leaders respect and honor authority but are comfortable in its presence.

$\mathcal{Y}$ou have to choose to fulfill your leadership nature. Having the leadership spirit without the spirit of leadership is like having a powerful automobile without the knowledge or ability to drive it. It is like a seed that never becomes the tree it was destined to be.

Our attitudes cannot stop our feelings, but they can prevent our feelings from stopping us.

A poor self-image or self-concept will always result in a low valuation of humanity and will become the source of abuse, corruption, oppression, and the need to dominate and control others.

*N*othing is more dangerous than power in the hands of one who suffers from a sense of mental inferiority. The formula for oppression is power without mental soundness.

$\mathcal{I}$f you love yourself in the true sense, you'll always use your power to help other people rather than to harm them. How you see yourself is how you will see everyone else you relate to. You cannot love anyone beyond your love for yourself.

The essence of leadership is that you give other people value. In other words, you give them something valuable to contribute to and become involved in. True leadership provides people a cause, a reason for living, and a sense of significance that gives meaning to their lives so that they feel necessary and purposeful.

$\mathcal{Y}$ou cannot give significance if you don't already have it. You cannot lead people where you have not gone yourself.

$\mathcal{T}$he value you place on others is a reflection of the value you place on yourself.

*Y*ou must come to the point where you are convinced that you are necessary. True leaders believe that they are necessary—they know they are needed by their generation and the world.

The beliefs and convictions of a leader regulate the nature of his leadership.

What you believe in your heart is essential, vital, crucial to your life. You live out of your heart. You see through your heart. You interpret through your heart. You judge through your heart. You lead out of your heart.

*I*f you do not erase or replace the "corrupt" information about leadership you have taken into the "hard drive" of your heart, then your leadership will be distorted. True leadership demands a constant monitoring of what goes into your heart.

True leadership is manifested when one individual uses his or her flame to light the lives of many and help them discover the reservoir of hidden oil in their lamps.

*Y*our attitude is more powerful
than your reputation.

KEYS for LEADERSHIP

Your ability to lead depends
on the attitude produced by your
self-image and self-esteem.

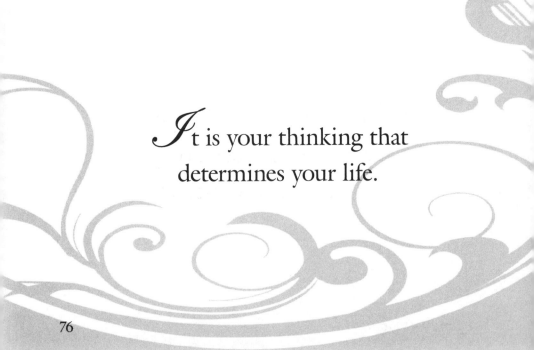

*I*t is your thinking that determines your life.

What we do not know about ourselves limits us. Leaders are limited by the extent of their knowledge of the truth about themselves and the world.

$\mathcal{T}$rue leadership has more to do with mind-set than with methods and techniques.

$\mathscr{B}$eing a leader is a natural part of our makeup, but thinking like a leader is difficult.

$\mathcal{T}$raining in leadership really means training in attitude because attitude has to do with how we respond to life. We must think, talk, walk, dress, act, respond, decide, plan, work, relate, and live like a leader.

*I*n my experience, leadership is 20 percent talent, skill, and technical knowledge, and 80 percent attitude.

$\mathcal{C}$ultivating the spirit of leadership is a choice, and only you can make it.

You will always act in a way that is consistent with your self-image.

*H*ow you define yourself is the single most important statement you can make about yourself, and it is the heart of attitude. The spirit of leadership will emerge from your self-definition.

*A*ttitudes are nothing more than habits of thought produced by your self-image, self-worth, and self-esteem. These habits can be acquired and changed by the reconditioning of the mind.

True leadership cannot be born or exist without a sense of purpose.

$\mathcal{P}$urpose creates a leader because it provides an assignment for life and signals a sense of significance.

$\mathcal{Y}$our leadership is hidden in your purpose, and your purpose is the key to your passion.

The attitude of passion is an indispensable
attribute of leadership and serves as
the driving force of motivation that
sustains the focus of the leader.

To become the leader you were created to be, you must find a purpose for your life that produces a passion for living.

$\mathcal{L}$eaders don't just do, they *feel* what they're doing. Their passion continually motivates and inspires them.

*T*rue leaders don't have jobs;
they have lifetime assignments.

*L*eadership is born when one discovers
a divine obligation to his community,
world, and generation.

$\mathscr{L}$eaders are willing to put their whole selves into accomplishing their purposes.

True leaders are resolved in their decisions to pursue their goals and purposes.

*P*assion helps us to rise above
our daily routines.

*T*rue leaders do not need outside
stimuli in order to take action.
They are self-motivated.

*I*f you capture a sense of destiny that existed before you and will continue to exist after you, and if you feel you're involved in something that is larger than yourself, you're on your way to leadership. Passion is born when you connect to both the past and the future.

Keys for Leadership

A leader usually moves toward things that can't yet be seen but will be manifested in the future.

A true leader builds *on* the past
and *for* the future.

$\mathscr{L}$eaders know that purpose is much bigger than one incident or several incidents. They keep on moving toward the fulfillment of their purposes, no matter what.

*Y*ou know your vision is from God when you are still at it once the storm clears.

Leaders don't wait for the future to come; they create it. They don't wait for others to do what they know they should or could do.

*L*eaders don't just dream; they awaken and act on their dreams.

The attitude of initiative enables you to be your own coach so that you maintain momentum in pursuit of your life's purpose.

$\mathcal{N}$othing can be accomplished unless a decision has been made concerning it.

$\mathscr{W}$e often hesitate to take initiative because we are afraid of responsibility or the consequences of our actions.

*B*e a leader—initiate.

All true leaders are distinguished by their strong sense of priorities.

What we do determines who we are and what we become. True leaders have a clear sense of what they need to do.

*E*ffective leadership involves the management of one's priorities. True leaders have learned how to distinguish between what is truly important for their lives and the fulfillment of their purposes and what is an urgent but temporary need.

We can do many things, but not everything is constructive to our lives. One of our major responsibilities as leaders is determining what is best for ourselves according to our life's purpose and vision.

True leaders make a distinction between an opportunity and a distraction, between what is good and what is right for them. Leaders know that priorities protect energy, time, resources, and talent.

$\mathcal{A}$ll true leaders possess a goal-driven attitude. Leaders distinguish themselves from followers by their passion for preestablished goals.

A leader understands how to set the
right goals. This is a vital attitude to cultivate
because your future and your life depend
on the goals you set—either consciously or
subconsciously. Where you end up in
life is a result of the goals that you
set or did not set for yourself.

Goals protect us from undue influence from other people. True leaders are always zealous for and jealous of their goals because these goals represent their lives. Our lives change when our goals change, so we must carefully guard our goals.

*I*f you don't have any goals, other people will run your life.

A goal is an established point for achievement that leads to a greater accomplishment.

$\mathscr{A}$ goal is a prerequisite for the achievement of an ultimate plan.

Goal setting is the art of discipline.

Goals create targets for our energy.
They protect us from procrastination.

 eaders...

- state their goals.
- communicate their goals.
- are committed to their goals.
- are regulated by their goals.
- are disciplined by their goals.
- stick to their goals.
- believe in their goals.
- focus on their goals.

$\mathcal{L}$eaders...

- measure their progress and
  success by their goals.

- revise their goals when necessary.

- protect their goals from interference
  and distraction.

- transfer their goals to their coworkers
  and the next generation.

The secret to leadership success is living a very focused life in line with your purpose.

*T*rue leaders possess the attitude of teamwork because they do not care who gets the credit.

A leader is always a team player. True leaders are cognizant that no great accomplishment has ever been achieved by one individual.

A leader understands that every person was created to fill a need. Everyone has an ability that no one else has and is indispensable in the world.

$\mathscr{B}$ecause of their unique gifts and perspectives, each human being is a solution to a certain problem that needs to be solved.

*I*nnovation is the creative reserve of true leaders.

The spirit of leadership is always manifested in an innovative attitude. The very nature of leading demands an innovative spirit as leaders take followers to an as-yet undiscovered world of vision.

True leaders learn from their experiences, but they never live in them. They never live their lives by prior experiences or they would become entrenched in the past. Leaders don't allow the past to dictate or entrap the future.

*T*rue leaders are never
prisoners of tradition.

$\mathcal{H}$aving a predetermined mind-set hinders the leadership spirit of innovation.

*W*henever you encounter a project, a challenge, or a problem, practice thinking in new ways and with a different mind-set.

$\mathcal{H}$arness creativity and explore the uncharted worlds of the untested.

$\mathcal{L}$eaders don't follow paths—they create trails. Leaders venture where others don't dare to tread.

Venture into the uncomfortable zone—innovate.

The spirit of true leadership always
possesses a sense of accountability
and responsibility.

$\mathscr{T}$rue leaders are conscious of their stewardship of the trust given to them by those whom they serve. The spirit of leadership seeks to be faithful to the sacred trust of the followers rather than doing what will please the leader.

The protection of leadership is in a voluntary submission to a trusted authority. The spirit of accountability is the active manifestation of submission to authority.

$\mathcal{B}$e cognizant that whatever you do as a leader may be personal, but it is never private. Be aware of your ultimate accountability to the Creator of all leaders.

The spirit of leadership never gives up until it achieves its goal; it is a spirit that never quits.

$\mathscr{L}$eaders persist because they have a firm grasp of their purposes, know where they are going, and are confident that they will arrive there.

$\mathcal{T}$rue leaders believe that the attainment of their purposes is not optional, but rather an obligation and a necessity, so they would never think of giving up.

*G*enuine leaders
understand that self-discipline is
the manifestation of the highest form of
government—self-government.

The true spirit of leadership cultivates a self-control that regulates one's focus and orders one's life. The disciplined lifestyle distinguishes leaders from followers.

$\mathscr{L}$eaders know that the most powerful kind of control is self-control because it is the hardest to master but reaps the greatest rewards. Therefore, they are more concerned about controlling themselves than controlling other people.

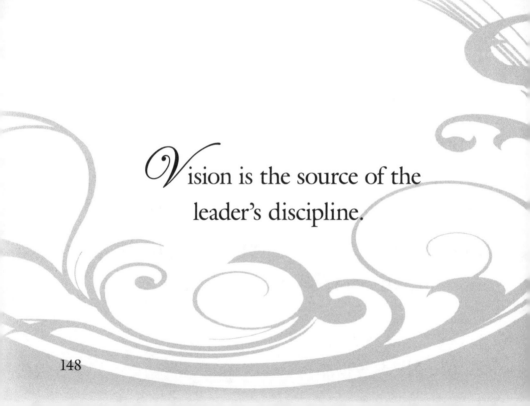

*V*ision is the source of the leader's discipline.

*A*ll true leaders are students *of* life and *for* life.

*T*rue leaders possess the leadership attitude of self-cultivation, a passion for personal development.

$\mathcal{L}$eaders are always looking for opportunities to advance their knowledge. They create their own learning opportunities and facilitate their own educational environments. A leader's personal collection of books is usually his greatest possession.

$\mathcal{L}$eaders study beyond the realm of their own disciplines—but in ways that will advance their purposes and visions.

The leadership attitude is more concerned with fully expressing itself than with attempting to prove itself to others.

$\mathscr{L}$eadership is both an art and a science:
it is innate and yet learned; it is inherent
and yet must be developed.

Keys for Leadership

$\mathscr{T}$rue leadership is the hope of the future of our world and will determine the success or failure of our homes, communities, cities, nations, and planet.

$\mathcal{L}$eadership is the only thing that will fulfill our innate passion for greatness.

Genuine leadership is the discovery of one's purpose and assignment for life and the inherent gifts and abilities that come with that assignment. It is the commitment to serve your gift to the world in order to enhance the lives of many.

ABOUT THE AUTHOR

*D*r. Myles Munroe is an international motivational speaker, best-selling author, educator, leadership mentor, and consultant for government and business. Traveling extensively throughout the world, Dr. Munroe addresses critical issues affecting the full range of human, social, and spiritual development. The central theme of his message is the transformation of followers into leaders and the maximization of individual potential.

Founder and president of Bahamas Faith Ministries International (BFMI), a multidimensional organization headquartered in Nassau, Bahamas, Dr. Munroe is also the founder and executive producer of a number of radio and television programs aired worldwide. He has a B.A. from Oral Roberts University, an M.A. from the University of Tulsa, and has been awarded a number of honorary doctoral degrees.

Dr. Munroe and his wife, Ruth, travel as a team and are involved in teaching seminars together. Both are leaders who minister with sensitive hearts and international vision. They are the proud parents of two college graduates, Charisa and Chairo (Myles, Jr.).

THE ISLANDS OF THE
bahamas

For Information on Religious Tourism
e-mail: ljohnson@bahamas.com
1.800.224.3681

www.worship.bahamas.com

These inspirational quotes from best-selling author Dr. Myles Munroe
on leadership, single living, marriage, and prayer can be applied
to your life in powerful and practical ways.

Keys for Leadership:	ISBN: 978-1-60374-029-6 • Gift • 160 pages
Keys for Living Single:	ISBN: 978-1-60374-032-6 • Gift • 160 pages
Keys for Marriage:	ISBN: 978-1-60374-030-2 • Gift • 160 pages
Keys for Prayer:	ISBN: 978-1-60374-031-9 • Gift • 160 pages

WHITAKER
HOUSE

www.whitakerhouse.com